South First and Lakefront

South First and Lakefront

poems by
Dennis Herschbach

Lost Hill Books
Duluth, Minnesota

Copyright 2010
Lost Hills Books and Dennis Herschbach.
All rights reserved.

This work may not be reproduced or transmitted, in whole or in part, without the written permission of the author.

ISBN 13: 978-0-9798535-5-5

Published by:
Lost Hills Books
P.O. Box 3054
Duluth, MN 55803
www.losthillsbks.com

Cover photo: Diane Hilden
Cover design: Aaron Bosanko
Interior layout: Aaron Bosanko

Manufactured in USA

Contents

Foreword i
Wilderness Silence. 1
Through My Lens. 2
The Corner of South First and Lakefront 3
One Street Up From South First 5
One Street Down From South First 7
Hard Climb to North Fourth 9
Secret Lives 11
A World Away From South First 12
Third Street 14
Nothing Left 16
Sunday Morning. 18
Dance to Nowhere. 20
At the Art Gallery 22
A Pharisaic View. 24
The Yin and the Yang 26
Hope 27

Foreword

Gradually, in the decades following Shakespeare's departure, the city began to replace the castle as the locus both of power and treachery, a shift quite naturally reflected in the settings and themes of our literature. London replaced Ellsinore, and lyric poetry, not to mention the novel, turned toward a critique of city life. One of the fine Twentieth Century moments in this tradition is the "Preludes" of T.S. Eliot—short, linked poems that offer snapshots of a grim, de-spiritualized environment, London again, in which time leaves a trail of "the burnt out ends of smoky days."

Dennis Herschbach's new collection follows in this tradition, giving it a uniquely American treatment. His poems present glimpses of, and meditations on, a city: glimpses through the eyes of a man who walks the streets and records impressions and feelings, who imagines desperate lives behind drawn shades and who witnesses street violence that doesn't bother to hide itself....

In his chapbook, *South First and Lakefront*, Herschbach captures a side of city life that is at once cynical and realistic.

The city can be any city; they are all quite alike, with neighborhoods for the well to do, working class locations, business districts, churches, hospitals, and, yes, a bowery with its bars and taverns.

I suppose anyone reading this collection can transpose the scenes so they correspond to their favorite waterfront city.

For example, if Lakefront were to be turned into Lake Avenue, and if South First were rotated ninety degrees it might become First Street. If those changes were made, the city might be Duluth, Minnesota.

Imaginative readers will be able to play similar games with their own familiar towns.

Herschbach has chosen to concentrate his writing on the supposition that all people have their frailties. Perhaps we are more similar to each other than we care to admit. We all need people in our lives. We all seek happiness and security. At times, we all have the need to escape. Some find escape in a bottle. Some find escape in less destructive ways.

In *South First and Lakefront*, Herschbach has captured the despair of the homeless, the peace of a city park, the struggle by some to survive, the hypocrisy of a few but in the end, hope, even for the hopeless.

Bruce Henricksen

Wilderness Silence

I've heard deep silence
as total as blackness
of a moonless night
that swallows echoes
before they bounce
from rock cliff
sounding boards.

Firefly flashes punctuate
the bottomless darkness
like pinpoints of sound
from a cricket's
fiddling chirp, or the lonely
whoo-hooing of an owl.

Silence, an empty abyss
ahead of storm clouds,
a black curtain torn
by serrate lightning
before thunder shatters peace
into splintered shards
like midnight sounds
of an inner city street
where the moon is erased.

Neon lights, blaring signs,
streams of energy punctuated
by pinpoints of silence,
each snuffed by sounds:
the impatient honk of horns,
screams of tires on hot tar,
a handgun's staccato bark
in a back alley.

Through My Lens

My stories walk the streets,
circle South First
and Lakefront
like birds trying to land,

trying to find a perch where lives
play out in hope
as fragile as flowers
in cracks of a broken wall,

where our worlds meet, and I
pass by,
watch
through un-tinted glasses

vignettes acted out by players,
each person a scene
from one act
of an endless drama.

Like a keen-eyed vulture
on a parapet wall,
I read their stories
as though they are carcasses

waiting for me to pick
their dead bones clean.

The Corner of South First and Lake Front

Ten in the morning and down the street
a flower shop's unlocked,
a rubber wedge props the door open
for flies and customers. The owner
fluffs bedraggled chrysanthemums,
peels petals from week old roses,
quenches the thirst of wilting plants.

Across the street, a peppermint pole
corkscrews its way into the air;
the barber sweeps up yesterday's hair,
spins the chair for the first cut.
He asks how the ballgame went,
how the war is going, if wife
and family are doing well,
what with the heat and all.

Ten in the morning, the cabbie
stops for a fare, loads a leather bag
branded with scrapes and scars
into the trunk of a dented, yellow taxi.
The meter clicks off every minute
one dollar at a time,
and the driver asks, "Where to?"

A couple stops where the sign reads,
"VACATIONS," wishing they
could dive into the poster picture
of white sand beaches and azure water.
They plan to escape from South First.

Ten in the morning and on the corner
two bleary men lean on the wall

of the tavern that might not have closed
at closing time, and one vomits;
the other laughs,
still lost in his bottle.
Inside, the dayshift mops.

   ****

Two in the afternoon, she stumbles out
in her ankle-length nightgown,
steadies herself on the bus stop sign,
hikes the fabric to her waist, her triangular
yield sign black against white skin
seldom touched by tanning rays,
and amber relief splashes on bare feet.
She ceremoniously lets go the hem,
wobbles back with self-observed dignity.

   ****

Nine at night and neons flicker.
Down the street, the green letters
announce F OWERS FOR ALE.
The peppermint pole has stopped
corkscrewing its way to nowhere,
and there are no cabs to hail.
Vacations wait behind CLOSED.

   *****

One in the morning and on the corner
two men break another's face; his blood
paints over gutter's yellow stain.
Sixty-two cents roll from his pocket.

Ten in the morning and down the street…

One Street Up From South First

Ten in the morning and down the street
clones in gray suits and striped ties,
black skirts and matching tops,
queue up at counters to order
five-dollar-a-shot mocha lattes.
They carry today's edition
of the *Journal* under one arm,
dangle genuine kangaroo leather
cases holding assets and others' dreams.

Across the street a boutique's unlocked,
its door inviting the invited. The owner
dresses mannequins in high heels
and plunging necklines, necklace
pendants to draw eyes between.

Ten in the morning, papers shuffle
on desktops and trophy nameplates
crow success. Millions shift
in a find the pea game; hucksters
move virtual walnut shells at
slight-of-hand speed leaving no trail,
and everything disappears.

****

Two in the afternoon and she primps
in front of the ladies' lounge mirror
preparing the bait for another catch,
ceremoniously saunters out,
trailing pheromones that make
him weak kneed and bleary.

****

– 5 –

Nine at night and neons flicker
HI TON above the city street.
He pours her a sherry aperitif.
She bares her black triangle,

tanned skin tattooed
with a string bikini line.
They yield.

With self-observed dignity
she dresses, smoothes wrinkles
in her character by combing
tangles from her hair, replaces
smudged lipstick at the mirror,
wonders who it is looks back.
He leaves his tie crooked;
he might have worked late.

       ****

Midnight, and he slithers into bed,
moves his wife's arm,
withers on his side of the bed
when she rolls over to him,
whispers, "You work too hard,"
kisses the back of his head
and sleeps until seven.

       ****

Ten in the morning and down the street…

One Street Down From South First
(Nightshift on the Docks)

Ten in the evening:
the whistle blows, harbor lights
reflect off water, current spins,
folds on itself, pours through
the canal entry, carries city mess
into the Great Lake. An ore carrier,
Roger Blough, plows against the flow,
makes its way to Dock Five, empties
muddy ballast into night-black swells,
readies to take on pellets bound
east to hungry furnaces of steel mills,
and she bends and groans in protest
to the tonnage in her belly.
Across the harbor, *Thomas Wilson*,
stranded dry in the dock,
sits high on timbers. Sweating welders
run molten beads upon her hull.
Angle grinders spray sparks,
shaping steel to make her float.

Two in the morning:
workers peel off gloves,
shielding masks, and greasy caps,
let nighttime run its fingers
through their hair, gather sounds
of a living pier close to their chests.
They eat cold sandwiches,
drink hot coffee,
talk of last night's game,
the wife and kids, NASCAR racers,
listen to the night's voice
call them back to the ship they will
tend to for the next five hours.

<u>Five in the morning:</u>
in the east, a thin line of pink
separates lake from air, and an arch
of blazing red rises to chase away
the veil of fog specters that dance
and pirouette on the watery stage.

<u>Seven in the morning:</u>
the whistle blows

Hard Climb to North Fourth

It's a hard climb from South First,
with each step the sidewalk rises,
meets her foot, and the
tilted earth holds her back.
She drags a loaded two wheeled cart,
strap, securing a bag of groceries
and a coat so worried both
elbows are worn through,
frayed edges fringe back
into worn weave.
Two steps, sometimes one,
a pause to rest, five breaths,
two more steps—or one ...
I want to run to her, to say,
"Here! Let me help!"

The traffic light signals "go."
I follow the flow south,
turn right on First, pass the casino
where Cadillacs wait in line
and valets open doors
for grey-haired men and
women in short-hemmed dresses
with necklines that plunge to their waists.

No one notices yet another old lady
wearing shoes with heels worn crooked,
her dress hem matching her limp.
She pulls a two-wheeled cart.
The traffic light holds up its red hand,
I stop. She hobbles along,
almost unnoticed.

A glacier of cars funnels

through narrow streets,
creeps along under its own weight.
My conscience takes the wheel,
I turn left, then left again.

She's standing at North Fourth,
leaning on her man.
His boney, vein-lined hand holds hers,
the other holds their two wheeled cart.
They smile a lover's smile
into the fleeting day.

Secret Lives

Evening shades are drawn down low;
only the shadows show what goes on
in secret places on the other side.

A line of backlit windows
hide a story of many rooms.
A lighted door says welcome
to summertime-warmth—
or winter-frigid night.

The next house on the avenue,
its view obscured by heavy drapes,
spills slivers of light that
trickle through narrow slits
onto an arid concrete walk.

Next door, all lamps are out.
Darkness hangs about, and stillness
wraps comfort arms around
mute cold stone walls.
Do lovers lie in each others' arms—
or is the home abandoned?

What goes on behind thick veils,
a mystery to those who glance
and we wonder at the shadows,
secrets held tight by those inside.

We walk the streets,
our inner shades drawn low.

A World Away from South First

From where the boulevard snakes
around the escarpment's jagged edge,
South First is an asphalt thread
gathering late summer heat that radiates
in rippling thermal waves off broiling tar.

From up here, I see buses stop
at measured intervals, shining
automated dots weave in and out,
ants scurry on pencil-line sidewalks.

Down there, two men share a bottle
from a brown paper bag, see the world
as if they're looking into water
of a fast flowing stream that distorts,
like the one that runs crystal clear
high behind Sky Line Drive,
where Chester Creek channels
over jumbled rock,
spills through narrow gates,
swirls, eddies, splashes
its way under leaning maples.
In early autumn they drop leaves,
paper thin parachutes that drift
to the water, land without a sound.

Reds, browns, yellows twirl and dance
in the current, gracefully waltz
in quiet pools, are caught up
by the beat of water jitterbugging
over slippery river rock, then are
washed along at a march's pace
until they're carried out of sight.

Old men sit in the shade,
gnarled knuckles resting
on wooden canes.
Children flush frogs
from grassy banks, chase them
into knee deep water,

and parents know
these days are too few left.

Lovers touch, just a shoulder rub
that promises more tonight,
feel the other's thoughts,
decide to take a long walk.

Third Street

St. Mary's Hospital

Noon, and the chimes
of the Catholic church
call twelve times.
No one hears, and Mary

stands riveted
to the hospital wall,
her face cast down,
a tarnished bronze halo

suspended above her
holy head, cold
in the January freeze.
On the first floor

my blood runs cold through
a machine, cold enough
that I'll not die when they cut
my chest, peel me open,

stop my heart
so they can hold it
in their hands,
along with my life

that will be returned
when they are done,
returned to its cage,
returned to its rhythm

of fill and empty,
push and rest
lub and dub.

Cadence

that signals wholeness
under bloody gloves
of the surgical team.
Across the street

the chimes call six.
Jesus, standing in the lobby
as still as carved marble,
looks at his wounded hands

while outside and around the corner
a homeless teen warms
hers under the exhaust vent
of the operating room.

Nothing Left

It runs almost dry in the fall;
miserly trickles between rocks
drip over bedrock ledges,
disappear into fine crushed gravel,
emerge on gray slate shelves.
In glassine sheets that spill

over polished slabs of flag,
it runs. Almost dry in the fall,
a liquid ribbon serpentines
behind round boulders,
in front of gabbro shards.
An almost vanished stream

writhing its way along,
withering, dying.
It runs almost dry. In the fall,
before October rains spill
from steely skies,
the anemic rivulet flows,

follows paths carved by eons
of grinding grit that maps
a destined twisted route.
It runs almost dry in the fall,
a river that once danced
and skipped down to the lake,

roared and spewed spray
into the sunshine making
rainbow arcs above the chaos
of churning water. But now,
it runs almost dry in the fall,
like someone thirsting,

someone whose life
is an empty stream:
the derelict on South First
wasting away in shadows,
his river of hope all but gone.
It runs almost dry in the fall.

Sunday Morning

Ten-thirty, and in the suburbs
families turn respectable,
men dress in white shirts
and subtle ties, kids comb
their hair, women spray perfume,
and they drive a few blocks
in their SUV, park between
a Lexus and black Audi.

Greeters smile and shake
their hands, comment that
they look so nice this morning.
Reality hides behind painted smiles,
and they are ushered into polished
hardwood pews, the same place
they sat last week, the week before.

Preacher, in his white robe,
proper colored vestment
with matching cincture
pronounces their sins are forgiven,
and they sing hymns, hear about
feeding His sheep, and they
have done their duty for the week.

A mile away near the corner
of South First and Lake Front,
doors with brown peeling paint
open to the street. *Gospel Mission*
reads the sign over the portal.
From somewhere in its labyrinth halls,
good smells sneak out the door:
hamburger gravy cooking in a caldron,
steamed beans simmering in a pot.

Men, some wearing holey shirts
escaping their ragged belts,
others hung over, needing a shave,
straggle in, and a few women wearing
their own odor. They take seats
on sliver-ridden wooden benches,
sing a hymn in tune to an out of tune

chord organ, bow their heads
at the proper time, and hear
a message about a prodigal saved.
A prayer of thanksgiving,
and the sheep get fed.

In the suburbs, a child asks Dad
if they can get a sheep.

Dance to Nowhere

Down by the canal,
music grinds on at a weary
TA-*ta-ta*-**TA**-*ta-ta*-**TA** pace,
beginning a dance to nowhere.
Eyes leer; some in groups,
others alone, far back
at tables hid in shadows.

Blank gaze seeks places
far distant from this stage,
somewhere she is not.
Surreal faces disappear;
smoky fog banks create screens
her mind can hide behind.
Not seen, they don't exist.

Thoughts cease to form;
beat penetrates depth of soul.
Rhythm propels movement
to mind dead body.
Senses numbed from being merchandized:
living commodity for sale –
what's *it* worth?

Music plays with no emotion;
dancer follows until time
for show don't tell is over –
for a while.

Tepid applause,
weak sign of appreciation,
whatever.

Dance ends
with sagging breasts,
deep-lined skin,
man-handled emotions.

At the Art Gallery

I stared at her;
she looked back
like she didn't care,
eyes averted, unseeing,
holding a long kept secret,
leaving me wondering
what she thought.

I moved to the next,
an oil on canvass by Steen
where the housewife sleeps,
pigs eat off the kitchen floor,
and the household crumbles.
I wait for her to move,
to do something, anything.

Next, a harvest scene
of flaxen haystacks,
meandering rail fences,
women reaping grain,
all seen through Van Gogh's
detailed perceptive eye.
I try to see what he saw.

A Vermeer takes me
to a time when milkmaids
poured warm, fresh milk
from earthen pitchers,
tables held heavy breads
waiting for yellow edams,
fresh churned butter.

Delicate young girls
sit under trees that shaded

Renoir as he dabbed paint,
forgetting to dress his models,
creating pubescent portraits
unlike Girl in the Picture Frame
captured by Rembrandt,

her facial features
accentuating eyes so dark
I drown in their depth,
brown hair dusting her neck
and a childlike mouth
waiting for the right kiss.
There is a Monet,

muted colors blended,
forming a quiet scene
of faceless, nameless strollers
promenading the boulevard,
nondescript Parisians
lost in their own world
of featureless obscurity.

I am alone under the exit sign.
A revolving door spins me out
to a crowd on the street,
people whose faces
might well have been
painted by Monet.

A Pharisaic View

From the parkway, he looks down,
sees ten thousand lights of the city.
Streams of red streak away,
follow charted paths.
White points of light meteor in

at lowly mortals,
those people in their houses
who work and love,
rest and hate and die
in obscurity of smallness

where nothing matters.
Walls and fences
and commonness
anathema to him,
a chasm he will not cross,

and *their* night
belongs to bar fights,
fear-filled alleys,
peddlers of passion,
flop houses.

Down there, sirens whine,
jackhammers ratchet,
car horns honk
silencing silence in the crush
of infused chaos.

From up here, he looks down,
drinks in sights of his universe,
admires distant cities
lit up like galaxies,
and plays at being god.

The Yin and the Yang

Walk beside the lake
where brick-cobbled paths wind
between rose bush hedges,
and azaleas slump in the shadows
like barflies who have lost their bloom.

Follow paved trails canopied
by elms and ash that umbrella
the few park benches
where readers read, lovers love,
homeless live.

Stop where the monument shell
spreads its wings like a bird
protecting chicks, and read
dead names on the stone stele.

Run fingers over
smooth gray coolness
of polished rock
granite that speaks peace
to a world tangled in war.

Watch children build sand castles
on the beach, dream
of riding cloud animals
racing the wind in the sky.

Cradle their innocence,
a thin-shelled egg.

Find that place within yourself
where hope and hopelessness
sit on a balance
waiting for a nudge.

Hope

A block past the corner
of South First and Lake Front
a wall built of hand hewn stone
blocks the push of earth
that would slump onto the walk.

It's held its ground for ninety years,
but now is tired, some parts
fallen out, others flaking spalls
that fall where vagrants slouch,
their eyes seeing the world
through the curved glass
of an empty wine bottle.

There are cracks in the wall,
crevasses where dirt collects,
where a seed or two has settled.

From those seeds a plant
or two have sprouted, struggling
to survive with the survivable.
One stretches its face to the sun
and blooms, its petals fragile,
a little withered.

One person, in that instance
when the bottle is held just so,
sees the flower for what it is.

About the Author

Following the death of his wife, Dennis Herschbach published a book of prose and poetry, *Grief Journey*, in 2007. In 2010, he published a boyhood memoir, *BrownSugar Syrup and Jack Pine Sand*. Between books, Herschbach had several poems and short stories published, and he has won several awards for his poetry.

Herschbach currently resides in Two Harbors, Minnesota where he has lived since 1965.

Lost Hills Books
www.losthillsbks.com

NORMANDALE COMMUNITY COLLEGE
LIBRARY
9700 FRANCE AVENUE SOUTH
BLOOMINGTON, MN 55431-4399